SPIRIT CHANNEL-ING

Evaluating the Latest
in New Age Spiritism

BROOKS ALEXANDER

INTERVARSITY PRESS
DOWNERS GROVE, ILLINOIS 60515

InterVarsity Press is the book-publishing division of InterVarsity Christian Fellowship, a student movement active on campus at hundreds of universities, colleges and schools of nursing. For information about local and regional activities, write Public Relations Dept., InterVarsity Christian Fellowship, 6400 Schroeder Rd., P.O. Box 7895, Madison, WI 53707-7895.

Distributed in Canada through InterVarsity Press, 860 Denison St., Unit 3, Markham, Ontario L3R 4H1, Canada.

A shorter version of this pamphlet originally appeared in Christianity Today *magazine.*

All Scripture quotations, unless otherwise indicated, are from the Holy Bible, New International Version. Copyright © *1973, 1978, International Bible Society. Used by permission of Zondervan Bible Publishers.*

ISBN 0-8308-1105-2

Printed in the United States of America.

Library of Congress Cataloging-in-Publication Data
Alexander, Brooks, 1936-
    Spirit channeling: evaluating the latest in New Age spiritism/
Brooks Alexander.
        p.   cm. —(Viewpoint pamphlets)
        "Originally appeared in Christianity today magazine"—T.p. verso.
        Bibliography: p.
        ISBN 0-8308-1105-2
        1. Channeling (Spiritualism)—Controversial literature.
    2. Christianity and psychical research.   3. Bible and spiritualism.
    I. Title.   II. Series.
    BF1286.A44 1988
    133.9'1—dc19   *88-23403*
                                                                  CIP

14	13	12	11	10	9	8	7	6	5	4	3	2	1
99	98	97	96	95	94	93	92	91	90	89	88		

"Bashar" is an extraterrestrial.

"Mafu" is a highly evolved being from the seventh dimension, last seen on Earth when he incarnated as a leper in first-century Pompeii.

"Ramtha" is a 35,000-year-old ascended master—once a barbarian warrior-king, later a Hindu god, now beyond even deity itself.

"Lazaris" is a disembodied personality with no incarnations—a being with no past lives in his portfolio.

These are not characters from *Super-hero Comix* or a "Star Trek" episode. They are "entities." And these entities, with others like them, have helped to create a modern mass-mania—the so-called channeling craze.

Besides their general implausibility, these entities have three things in common: They have no physical existence (that is, they are "spirits" or "spirit beings"); they are mainly interested in dispensing their philosophy of life to human beings; and they operate through other humans to do so, temporarily assuming control of the body during a trance state. People who subject themselves to such entrancement and control are called "channelers," or simply "channels."

According to the channels, the function of the trance state is to disengage the mind from involvement with the space-time world by shutting out sensory input. The same effect is achieved by making the input of a single sense dominant and repetitive, as in the chanting of mantras. This state of disengaged attention permits contact with the nonsensory realm of spirits and also vacates control of the physical faculties for use by the spirits themselves. While the channel is in an entranced condition, the controlling spirit, or entity, will lecture, counsel, teach or otherwise advise its human audience. As the entity operates the channel's body, it comes through as a "new inhabitant," a distinct and different personality. As one channel put it, "Channeling is a form of voluntary possession."

Rush Hour of the Entities

How significant is this trend? When the *Los Angeles Times* published a major article on the phenomenon, they headlined it "The New, Chic Metaphysical Fad of Channeling." Is this just another diversion for New Age dabblers, or is it something more enduring?

The impact of channeling is easy to see, but difficult to assess. Its current high profile comes chiefly from celebrity endorsement. Stars of stage, screen and tube have given public testimonials about their spirit guides. Linda Evans (of "Dynasty") and Joyce DeWitt (formerly of "Three's Company") follow the guidance of Mafu, channeled by Penny Torres, a California homemaker. When Sharon Gless won an Emmy for her role in "Cagney and Lacey," she announced in her acceptance speech that her success was due to Lazaris, channeled by Jach Pursel, a California businessman. Shirley MacLaine consults Ramtha, channeled by J. Z. Knight, a Washington State homemaker and breeder of Arabian horses. Ramtha/Knight has also appeared on the "Merv Griffin Show." Other entity-channel teams have become local radio and television personalities.

Publicity alone is ephemeral. There is more to the trend than the fleeting favor of movie stars. There is extensive grassroots involvement as well. Channeled books are the top-selling titles in the growing occult and metaphysical market; many of them instruct readers how to contact their own spirit guides and become channels themselves.

The current wave of channeled publications was set in motion by the late Jane Roberts. During the early 1970s, Roberts was channel for the entity "Seth," author of *Seth Speaks* and numerous other books. Today hundreds of people claim to be channels for Seth.

The Seth books were a milestone because they were produced by Prentice-Hall, a respected general-market publisher. Earlier spirit scribes had mostly been printed by obscure specialty houses. When the Seth venture proved popular, more such writings began to appear from major publishers.

Authors also published spirit-dictated material under their own names. *Jonathan Livingston Seagull* was dictated to Richard Bach by an entity that appeared in the form of a bird. Bach claims that he simply wrote down the stream of thoughts and impressions that the entity poured into his mind. The book broke all publishing records since the legendary success of *Gone with the Wind* and topped the best-seller lists for over two years.

The sheer number of titles in print today is unprecedented. The major New Age/Occult bookstore in Berkeley has seven shelves of channeled material. Three of those shelves hold the "older" books—the *Urantia Book*, the *Aquarian Gospel*, the works of Edgar Cayce and so on. The remaining four shelves hold more recently published material. Those four shelves outsell the rest of the bookstore—which goes to show that there's a wide readership out there. There are even entity-influenced magazines. *Metapsychology: The Journal of Discarnate Intelligence* "mines the lode of wisdom and knowledge coming from trance mediumship."[1] *Spirit Speaks* presents an ongoing, channeled "symposium," in which different entities channel their responses to a featured topic.

MasterCard Metaphysics

The final evidence of channeling's impact is found on the bottom line: channeling pays. It pays big, for the simple reason that large numbers of people are willing to part with the price of admission, however steep. Pursuing channeled guidance can be expensive. And supplying it can be rewarding. A case in point is Lazaris, channeled by Jach Pursel. By Pursel's own declaration, Lazaris is a commercial entity as well as a spiritual one.

It costs $275 to partake of Lazaris's wisdom at a weekend seminar. Between 600 and 800 people fill each session, which means that Lazaris channels an average of $190,000 into the bank per weekend of transcendental discourse. Lazaris has a two-year waiting list for private consultations, at $93 per hour. Or you can reach out and touch Lazaris by phone at $53 per half-hour, billed to your Visa or MasterCard account. Audio tapes of Lazaris are available at $20 per set, videotapes at $60. Pursel also sells New Age items and art. He is co-owner of the "Illuminarium" gallery in Corte Madera, California. The gallery specializes in expensive crystal jewelry and visionary paintings. It grosses five million dollars a year.

A reporter once asked Pursel if he didn't think it incongruous that a "spiritual" entity like Lazaris should be preoccupied with acquiring material wealth. Pursel replied: "I find it strange that spiritual entities need fancy business cards, that they need press secretaries . . . yeah, I do. And I don't like it that that's happened." So far, however, he hasn't convinced Lazaris to alter his merchandising style. And he hasn't refused the sizeable income Lazaris makes: "You don't have to have a miserable life to be spiritual. You don't have to sacrifice everything for your spirituality. You can have everything—and be spiritual!"[2]

Profitability alone is no basis on which to offer a critique (if it were, the church would be in serious trouble), but it does illustrate how modern spiritism appeals to our acquisitive nature. It also shows the extent to which this new religious practice has penetrated mainstream culture. Lazaris/Pursel may seem extreme, but he is by no means unique. It has been estimated that over 1,000 active channels practice in the Los Angeles area alone.[3] Southern California may be "the land of a thousand channels," but it is only a focused version of what is happening more diffusely in other places.

Spirits with a Past
Channeling itself is no novelty. In fact, it is es-

sentially identical to old-fashioned trance mediumship, one of the most ancient practices known to humankind. Indeed, there is irony in the fact that this spiritual relic is the latest rage of our "secular" age, the hottest fad of the so-called New Age movement.

In recent centuries, secularism and scientism have conspired to demystify the universe, but they have not delivered on their promise to eradicate irrationality. Secularism has weakened Christianity, but not superstition; it makes the concept of "truth" distasteful and thereby makes falsehood exotic. By rejecting the supernatural, secularism becomes a veil of denial; beneath it, spiritual error grows in the dark, without hindrance or attention.

Therefore, in the modern world there have been periodic outbreaks of spiritistic enthusiasm. Interestingly enough, these outbreaks often coincide with periods of religious ferment and the rise of aberrant religious teachings.

The origins of modern spiritism can be traced to the activities of the Fox sisters in upstate New York in 1849. Margaret and Katie Fox began by hearing mysterious rappings in their house at Hydesville. They ended by becoming active spirit mediums and public celebrities. Their trances and spirit messages excited a wave of fascination that eventually reached across the Atlantic to England and Europe.

The next wave of spiritism began in the 1870s, a decade that also saw the founding of the Jehovah's Witnesses and the Theosophical Society. Mediums of the time introduced some new wrinkles, including "automatic painting" under spirit control and "materializations" of "ectoplasm," the barely visible substance of which spirits are allegedly made. Periodicals appeared that were exclusively devoted to the subject. It was during this period that the general interest in mediums and spirits sparked efforts to investigate the matter scientifically. The Dialectical Society was formed in London in 1869, and the Society for Psychical Research at Cambridge in 1882.

In the twentieth century, public interest in spiritism has continued to rise and fall in cycles. The appetite for spirit contact increases after each major war. Spiritism often has its strongest attraction for those who have suffered personal bereavement, and after a war it always gains in appeal and credibility.

Today we live in a time of continual war—

multiple, overlapping conflicts that have interruptions but no end. Death dominates the headlines and loss overshadows our lives. In an age that daily faces mass extinction from pestilence, pollution and nuclear war, it is no wonder that the spirits are back and busier than ever.

The Modern Outburst

It is clear we are now in the midst of another major outbreak of spiritism. The spirits are not only more active than before, but in our biblically illiterate society, they are finding more people who are eager to lend them an ear. An expanding audience not only believes in them, it also believes them; it not only accepts their existence, it accepts their guidance as well.

Many people assume they accept the Bible without having read it for themselves. Thus they are easily misled to believe that certain entities are the original New Testament figures returning to write a sequel to Scripture. Jesus himself is claimed as the source of *A Course in Miracles,* a three-volume work that uses biblical terminology while actually distorting biblical doctrine. The disciples of Jesus are also popular writers, especially "Saint John."

Not all entities claim a Christian perspective. Other literary entities include "Raphael," an extraterrestrial; "Ra," an ancient Egyptian; and "White Eagle," a Native American. There are travelers from other planets, dwellers in other dimensions, denizens of ancient and lost civilizations and the very gods themselves. And now there is *Messages from Michael,* written by a *collective* entity: "not a ghost, not a spirit, but an amassing of souls on a higher plane of existence"[4]—shades of "Legion" (Mark 5:9)!

To the casual observer, this renewed fascination with spirits and spirit contact seems to have exploded into prominence without warning. The mass media uniformly treat channeling as a fringe phenomenon that swelled to fad status overnight. Public perception was brought to instant focus in January 1987, when ABC-TV aired Shirley MacLaine's miniseries based on her own experience with channelers and entities. "Out on a Limb" was a startling, prime-time testimonial to MacLaine's occult conversion and her belief in spirit guides. Suddenly the subject intruded on our collective attention.

But that impression of suddenness is a media-projected illusion. The unnoticed reality is that spiritism has been steadily working its way into the mainstream of American culture for the last twenty years. The disturbing reality is that channeling is just the tip of an iceberg, the visible part of a much larger pattern. The sobering reality is that the new spiritism has moved beyond the weird and the supernatural into the normal and the mundane. Quietly but convincingly, the entities have been serving notice that they are back—to stay.

Are the Entities for Real?

But who (or what) are "they"?

What is the nature of channeled entities? Are they objectively real, but disembodied beings that exist in some ethereal realm? Are they fabrications?

There seem to be four basic options: (1) the entities are real and are telling us the truth about themselves; (2) the entities are real and are lying to us; (3) the entities are a "dissociative reaction," a mental dysfunction unrecognized as such; (4) the entities are a conscious fraud for the purpose of gain.

We can eliminate the first option because the entities' claims are plainly at odds with the biblical view of reality. In fact, many entities explicitly reject the Bible's message of sin and salvation. These entities, even if they claim to be Christ himself, call down upon themselves the apostle Paul's curse, "If anybody is preaching to you a gospel other than what you accepted, let him be eternally condemned!" (Galatians 1:9).

Another theory suggests that a channeler splits off part of his or her unconscious mind into a separate personality, which in turn is manipulated by an entity. That explanation allows for real entities as well as real pathology. It also illustrates that deception is basic to the channeling process, since the entities themselves have encouraged a very different view of their nature.

Thus, the full answer to our question could involve the second, third and fourth options at various times and in various combinations. After all, deception and derangement are among the known tools of demonic activity. We should not be surprised to see them turn up as items on the demonic agenda.

We would naturally expect channels to insist on the objective reality of their entities. Some do, but others are curiously ambivalent. Jach Pursel says, "I suppose Lazaris could be a different part of me, a 'higher' part of me or something. And, ultimately, I'd say, well, if you want to think that, fine. Because what really matters is the value you gain from it. And if talking to another part of me can help you improve your life, then have at it."[5]

That airy indifference to matters of factual accuracy apparently rubs off on followers. A successful corporate executive who lives in California's trendy Marin County says, "I can't say that Lazaris is really a disembodied spiritual guide. To me it doesn't matter, as long as he's truthful and helpful."[6] Ram Dass (also known as Dr. Richard Alpert) is one channeling fan who is also a psychologist, and therefore should be able to evaluate the phenomenon. But he, too, uses his confusion about the facts as an excuse to avoid the issue of interpretation. Writing about "Emmanuel," an astral-plane entity channeled by East Coast housewife Pat Rodegast, Ram Dass says: "From my point of view as a psychologist, I allow for the theoretical possibility that Emmanuel is a deeper part of Pat. In the final analysis, what difference does it really make? What I treasure is the wisdom Emmanuel conveys."[7]

Ram Dass is correct—in one sense. In the final analysis, it is the "wisdom" that counts, not the bearer of it. And in this case the wisdom is the earthly, natural, demonic wisdom talked of in James 3:15. That is enough to identify the phenomenon regardless of who the messenger is. As Robert Burrows, editor of publications for Spiritual Counterfeits Project, has pointed out, real entities do not have to be channeled for real lies to be told or real damage to be done.[8]

But is real damage done? We've determined that entities are influential, but what does that influence amount to? What is the actual impact on people?

Teachings from the Twilight Zone

The entities' primary tool is their teaching. They will mainly affect our collective psyche, the presuppositions of our popular world view. In simple language, fans of channeling adopt the understanding of God and reality that the entities teach them.

Just as mediumship is no novelty, neither is there anything new in the beliefs that attend it. From ancient times, spiritism has consistently been the source of communications that embody the essence of occult philosophy: Death is unreal; all is One; we are Divine Beings and can control Reality with our powers of Mind. It hardly needs pointing out that this glittering vision of possibilities bears a striking resemblance to the serpent's temptation of Eve in the Garden of Eden: "You will not surely die. . . . For God knows that when you eat of it your eyes will be opened, and you will be like God" (Genesis 3:4-5). The entities give us no additions to that agenda of deception. What they give us is a new aggressiveness in pushing it, and a new use of high-tech tools to push it with.

Shirley MacLaine's TV miniseries was a virtual occult catechism. In one breathtakingly blatant scene, MacLaine is initiated into the understanding that Divine Being and the Human Soul are one. She and her spiritual adviser stand on Malibu Beach with their arms flung open to the cosmos, shouting, "I am God! I am God! I am God!"

When Ramtha channeled in to the "Merv Griffin Show" in October of 1985, Merv wanted to know, "What is your most important message that you want everyone on this planet to hear?" Ramtha replied, "What is termed God is within your being. . . . And that which is called Christ is within your being. And when you know you are God, you will find joy."

Equally egregious examples can be culled from a random scanning of channeled material. The denial of death is a dominant theme, always implied and often expressed. The entities endlessly repeat the primal lie, the ancient threefold creed of error: There is no death; man is God; knowledge of self is salvation and power (see Genesis 3:4).

Today, that message is merchandised. Both message and messenger are commodities, items of commerce to be packaged, promoted and sold. The spirits have always been marketable, but the size of that market has been strictly limited. When spiritism reaches a critical mass of popularity, it graduates to a new level of commerce and becomes mass-marketable. In this way it roots itself in the very foundations of our consumer society. That in itself represents a quantum leap from the days when believing in spirits and going to seances was considered eccentric at best.

Today's spiritism, in contrast to that of the past, has enormous commercial potential, and commerce controls the shape and direction of mass culture. In his book *Masks of Satan,* Christopher Nugent says,

> The Molech of consumerism is king, and the first thing it consumes is conscience. As the idols descend we have a convergence of the culture and the occult, a kind of "occulturation." . . . I would conclude that our culture may be becoming so demonic as to render particular cults redundant and superfluous.[9]

Nugent's conclusion may seem overstated. But in view of the open merger of spirit contact, occult philosophy, mass media and high finance, it hardly seems fanciful.

Delusion and Judgment

Channeling is part of a larger trend that is intensifying and will probably continue to do so. It is easy to see why. Spiritism's powerful appeal caters simultaneously to the modern state of mind and fallen human nature. Spirit contact fits perfectly into the jiffy-solution mentality of our day. It's quick. It's morally undemanding. And above all, it provides a strong, immediate experience of the "beyond" to substitute for our alienation from God.

Spiritism, therefore, accelerates the process of spiritual decline toward apostasy and judgment, for it involves not only an active rejection of God, but an active embrace of his replacement. It is, as the prophets put it, "spiritual adultery" carried to completion. It is faithlessness fulfilled. The biblical language that deals with spiritism is a litany of loathing: It is called *evil, error, folly, falsehood, apostasy* and *abomination* (see, for example, Deuteronomy 18:9-14 and Revelation 22:15). In the Old Testament, those who indulge in it are considered defiled and deserving of exile or death. In the New Testament, spiritists are identified as opposers of the gospel and enemies of the truth. *Taboo* is not too strong a term for the ban that the Bible applies.

The Bible's rejection of spiritism is stated early and often. For Moses and the prophets, concourse with spirits was a horror and an abomination, because the spirits were the driving force behind the false religions in direct conflict and competition with God. The Old Testament unfailingly testifies that all idolatrous worship is demon worship and fellowship with unclean spirits (see Leviticus 17:7; Deuteronomy 32:17; 2 Chronicles 11:15; Psalm 106:37).

Therefore, every temptation to idolatry was demonic. Since Israel was encircled by idolatrous nations, its spiritual warfare was reflected in its earthly warfare—continual cultural and military struggle against near and distant neighbors.

Deuteronomy 18:9-14 is a remarkable passage known as the "list of the abominations." It clearly connects the idolatrous heathen cultures that surround Israel with their spiritism (demonism) and their occult practices, especially divination:

> When you enter the land the LORD your God is giving you, do not learn to imitate the detestable ways of the nations there. Let no one be found among you who sacrifices his son or daughter in the fire, who practices divination or sorcery, interprets omens, engages in witchcraft, or casts spells, or who is a medium or spiritist or who consults the dead. Anyone who does these things is detestable to the LORD, and because of these detestable practices the LORD your God will drive out those nations before you.

These verses also make clear that this "constellation of uncleanness" inevitably provokes the devastating judgment of God.

The sad case of King Saul illustrates just how devastating that judgment can be (see 1 Samuel 28, 31). Saul was chosen by God and gifted for the tasks of kingship. But Saul resisted God and, at length, rejected God. When the multitude of his provocations caused the Spirit of God to depart, Saul stood alone and unprotected against the powers of evil; unprotected, he fell.

Under the anointing of God, Saul had hounded mediums and spiritists out of the country or into hiding (1 Samuel 28:3). Yet, at the close of his career, in despair he sought out a survivor of his persecutions—the "witch" or "medium" of Endor. Through her he hoped to get the supernatural guidance that God had ceased to supply. He got a message indeed, but the message was that his judgment was at hand. Saul's crime in consulting the medium was his final offense against God (1 Chronicles 10:13). The very next day God's judgment was executed in Saul's military defeat and acted out in his subsequent suicide.

The New Testament reaffirms the Old Testament revelation that the gods of heathen idolatry are demons. In 1 Corinthians 10:19-20 Paul plainly says that there is a spiritual power and reality behind heathen worship, but it is demonic and not the divine power it claims to be.

Thus the idol-ridden pagan culture of late antiquity (even by its own description) was a world crawling with gods, ghosts, spirits and demons, as well as the inevitable oracles who claimed to "channel" them. Acts 16:16-18 records Paul's encounter with one such oracle—a "slave girl who had a spirit by which she predicted the future. She earned a great deal of money for her owners by fortune-telling" (v. 16). Paul cast out the spirit with a word of direct command in the name of Jesus Christ. It was a deliverance that her owners did not appreciate, since her demonic bondage had been highly profitable to them (Acts 16:19-24).

A Biblical Rationale

But can we apply the Bible's attitudes to modern spirit contact? Or should we even try? A lot of spirit channeling seems merely silly—a minor self-deception in the quest for emotional comfort, or just a substitute for boredom. So why all the fuss? Does this odd mix of lunacy, foolery and exploitation really deserve the all-out attack that the Bible delivers against it?

The answer is yes for several reasons, but chiefly because of its effect on people. The teachings of spiritism tend to dull a person's ability to comprehend God or respond to the gospel of salvation. The silliness of most spiritism is beside the point. If the teachings are believed, they will have their impact, whether they are uttered by a sage or a buffoon.

The thrust of most spirit messages is a denial of the reality of death and its function as judgment. Now the Bible clearly sees God's judgment (either present or impending) as a spur to conscience, which convicts us of our own wrongdoing (sin) and faces us with our need for repentance and redemption. In the midst of that moral and ethical tension, the gospel of God's forgiveness is good news indeed, and is easily seen as such.

But if death is denied and its spur of judgment is disarmed, then conscience becomes dull and finally dormant. Repentance makes no sense; redemption appears irrelevant; and salvation seems to have no meaning. The gospel falls on deafened ears. Thus the demonic message serves the demonic purpose. That connection is remarkable for its persistence and consistency in history, and its coherence and pervasiveness today.

For that reason, the Bible treats spiritism as more than an act of personal culpability. Spirit contact is a symptom that goes beyond the individual who practices it and becomes a sign of social decline.

The ultimate biblical metaphor for a corrupt society is "Babylon." In both testaments Babylon is "a haunt for every evil spirit" (Revelation 18:2). It is also, not incidentally, the home of wickedness, sorcery, enchantments and divination, as well as breathtaking spiritual pride, the climax of which is the claim to be divine (Isaiah 47; Revelation 17; 18).

The extent to which a society endorses or indulges in spiritism, therefore, is a spiritual thermometer. As a social symptom, widespread spiritism represents the final stage of a long process of spiritual decay. It is the terminal phase of a people's flight from God.

All sin provokes God's judgment. Advanced or developed sin provokes it more directly and immediately. Terminal sin provokes a final judgment—not meant to admonish or correct, but to cleanse and extirpate. Terminal conditions signal the imminence of termination.

The practice of spiritism is terminal because it represents the ultimate confusion of values. It trades humanity's privilege of intimacy with God for sheer fascination with a liar who secretly hates all that is human and all that humans hold dear.

It is also terminal because it represents the ultimate confusion of identity and the ultimate derangement of personhood—the image of God in which we are made. The spirits' greatest skill is that of impersonation. It has been suggested that the spirits have "the power of ransacking the minds of the living as well as the dead, thus almost interfering with the fixity of personality itself. If this sort of ransacking were possible on a general scale, what chaos would follow in the realms of the living!"[10]

It is no wonder, then, that spiritism provokes the rejection and judgment of God. Everything about it—its source, its message and its effects—declares that it is at odds with Reality and so cannot endure. It is a substitute, a counterfeit, a poison and a ticket to perdition. It has no place in eternity and no place in the life of a Christian.

Back to the Future, Forward to the Past

In that light alone, the current goings-on have an urgent relevance to our lives. Christ exhorted us to "interpret the signs of the times" (Matthew 16:3). Part of that discernment comes from understanding the spiritual currents of the age.

The new spiritism is only one of many tributary streams in the rising flow of occult influence. It is only one of many means by which the basic message is drummed into the popular mind. It has less significance in its own right than it does as a representative symptom—a milestone on the road to delusion.

Western culture seems to be relapsing once again into the spiritual and intellectual condition of ancient Rome. Franz Cumont's *Astrology and Religion among the Greeks and Romans* describes the crumbling classical world in terms that are indistinguishable from the New Age movement's vision of the future: "In the declining days of antiquity the common creed of all pagans came to be a scientific pantheism, in which the infinite power of the divinity that pervaded the universe was revealed by all the elements of nature."[11]

The resurgence of spirit channeling and the

advent of the New Age movement herald the repaganization of our culture. We are returning to a spirituality that is natural to fallen humankind. If channeled New Age occult cosmic humanism is the wave of the future, it is only because it has always been the way of the world.

The twilight is ending. Night is descending. And angels of light come dancing in the dark.

Notes

[1]Alan Vaughn, "Channeling," *New Realities* (January/February 1987), p. 43.

[2]"The Selling of the Spirits," Part 1 (a TV news documentary; San Francisco: KPIX, January 1987).

[3]Lynn Smith, "The New, Chic Metaphysical Fad of Channeling," *Los Angeles Times,* December 5, 1986.

[4]Chelsea Quinn Yarbro, *Messages from Michael* (New York: Berkeley, 1980), back cover.

[5]"The Selling of the Spirits," Part 2.

[6]Janet Ghent, "Dialing in on Spiritual Channels," *Oakland Tribune,* December 30, 1986.

[7]Clarus Backes, "New Age Religion," *Contemporary Magazine* in the Sunday edition of *The Denver Post,* May 3, 1987, p. 11.

[8]Robert Burrows, "At Issue," *SCP Journal* 7, no. 1 (1987), p. 5.

[9]Christopher Nugent, *Masks of Satan* (London: Sheed and Ward, 1983), pp. 178, 180.

[10]A. E. Wilder-Smith, *The Drug-Users* (Wheaton: Harold Shaw, 1969), p. 211.

[11]Franz Cumont, *Astrology and Religion among the Greeks and Romans* (New York: G. P. Putnam's Sons, 1912), p. 56.